Original title:
The Glow of Laughter's Horizon

Copyright © 2025 Swan Charm
All rights reserved.

Author: Johan Kirsipuu
ISBN HARDBACK: 978-9908-1-3466-6
ISBN PAPERBACK: 978-9908-1-3467-3
ISBN EBOOK: 978-9908-1-3468-0

Whispers of Joyful Dawn

The sun peeks over the hill,
Birds begin their sweet song,
The world awakens with thrill,
A new day where we belong.

Gentle breezes softly blow,
Carrying scents of fresh dew,
Nature's beauty starts to show,
As the sky turns bright and blue.

Flowers open, colors bloom,
Life bursts forth in vibrant hues,
Chasing away the night's gloom,
A canvas painted with views.

Hope dances on every leaf,
Promises whisper in the air,
Moments filled with love and belief,
In this dawn, life feels so rare.

Joy flows in the morning light,
Every heartbeat sings with cheer,
Together we embrace the bright,
Whispers of joy linger near.

Radiant Echoes of Laughter

Children play beneath the sun,
Their giggles float on the breeze,
In this moment, we are one,
Joyful echoes, hearts at ease.

Friends gather with stories to share,
Laughter weaving in the air,
Every chuckle, light as a feather,
Creating bonds that last forever.

In the park, the world feels bright,
Happiness twinkling in eyes,
Radiant smiles, a pure delight,
Chasing clouds and reaching skies.

Every joke, a spark of glee,
Filling souls with warmth, alive,
In laughter's dance, we all agree,
It's in these moments we thrive.

With each note of shared mirth,
Life's burdens are gently unfurled,
In the treasure of joyful worth,
Laughter echoes through the world.

Light that Dances in Delight

Golden rays break through the trees,
Flickering like a playful sprite,
Nature sways with gentle ease,
As shadows play in warm sunlight.

The river sparkles like a dream,
Glittering under the sky's embrace,
A symphony, a joyful theme,
As waves waltz with a lively grace.

Flowers sway in the warm caress,
Petals twirling in the light,
With each breeze, they do confess,
In this moment, all feels right.

Dance with nature, lose all care,
Let your spirit feel the flight,
In this world, joy is laid bare,
Embrace the light that dances bright.

As day yields to evening's glow,
Stars join in, the dark's delight,
A serenade from the below,
Where dreams take wing in the night.

Serenade of Sunlit Smiles

In the morning's tender hue,
Smiles arise, warm as the sun,
Each face shines, a vibrant view,
A serenade where we are one.

Happiness floats on the air,
Every laugh, a gentle note,
Whispers of love set everywhere,
Hearts entwined, our dreams afloat.

With each glance, the world feels bright,
Sunlit moments, pure and warm,
In this dance, there's sheer delight,
Together weathering any storm.

Hands held tight, we walk this way,
Finding joy in simple things,
In the embrace of a new day,
Feel the music that love brings.

Let the sunshine fill your soul,
With every step, let laughter ring,
In the beauty that makes us whole,
We'll sing the song of everything.

Harmonies of Laughing Shadows

In a dance of twilight hue,
Shadows stretch, they play anew.
Whispers blend with gentle breeze,
Softly laughing through the trees.

Echoes of a child's delight,
Chasing dreams into the night.
Laughter twinkles, pure and bright,
In the shadows, hearts take flight.

Moonlight weaves a silver thread,
Through the stories softly said.
In this world of giggles spun,
Harmony has now begun.

Flickering Flames of Joyful Surprises

From the hearth, a warmth does rise,
Crackling tales and bright surprise.
Flickering flames with dancing light,
Bring forth joy, dispel the night.

Each spark jumps with laughter bold,
Whispers of stories yet untold.
Moments caught in playful chase,
Every flicker, a smiling face.

In the glow, our dreams ignite,
Chasing shadows, feeling right.
Hearts entwined in celebration,
These moments, our foundation.

Journey Through Sparkling Laughter

Step by step, through laughter we tread,
An adventure where joy is spread.
Through meadows bright, our spirits soar,
In every giggle, we explore.

Bubbles rise from cheerful streams,
Following the path of dreams.
Under skies of azure hue,
Sparkling laughter, ever true.

With each turn, surprises wait,
Moments perfect, no need to debate.
Together, where heartbeats are free,
Our journey unfolds, joyfully.

A Glimpse of Glee at Dusk

As the sun dips low, shadows play,
Golden hues fade, giving way.
A gentle glee fills the air,
Nature whispers without a care.

Crickets sing their evening song,
In this magic, we belong.
Soft clouds dance in colors bright,
A glimpse of glee, pure delight.

Holding hands, we take a pause,
In this stillness, a cause for applause.
With hearts aglow, we embrace,
This dusky moment, our safe space.

Celestial Smiles at Twilight

Stars begin to gently glow,
Whispers of the night take flight.
Moonbeams dance on rivers slow,
Painting dreams in silver light.

Crickets sing a lullaby,
As shadows stretch and sigh in peace.
The horizon embraces the sky,
Where day and night find their release.

A canvas brushed with hues of gold,
Twilight's secrets softly share.
In this moment, hearts unfold,
Wrapped in love beyond compare.

Each blink of stars, a story told,
Of wishes whispered on the wind.
In the dusk, our souls are bold,
As night's adventure does begin.

Prism of Playful Euphoria

Colors burst in vibrant cheer,
Laughter weaves through light and shade.
In this moment, free from fear,
Joyous trails of dreams are laid.

Children's voices fill the air,
Chasing rainbows, hearts ablaze.
Every giggle, a sweet prayer,
Dancing through the summer days.

Butterflies in playful flight,
Weaving stories in the sun.
Nature's palette, pure delight,
In this dance, we all are one.

The world spins in hues so bright,
A prism made of love and grace.
In our hearts, the purest light,
Euphoria finds its rightful place.

Laughter's Soft Embrace at Dawn

Morning breaks with softest light,
Sunrise paints the sky anew.
Laughter warms the chilly night,
As dreams awaken, bright and true.

Gentle whispers fill the air,
Songs of birds begin to rise.
In this moment, free from care,
Hope ignites as spirits fly.

Dewdrops twinkle on the grass,
Nature's smile, a warm embrace.
In this beauty, time does pass,
Hearts united in this space.

With each laugh, the dawn fulfills,
Promises of a brand new day.
In the glow of morning's thrills,
We find ourselves along the way.

Daybreak of Unfettered Joy

Golden rays break through the haze,
A symphony of life begins.
With each step, our hearts ablaze,
In this dance, the spirit wins.

Waves of laughter crash and swell,
As the day unveils its charms.
In this joy, we know so well,
Safety nestled in its arms.

Fields of flowers, wild and free,
Nature's bounty calls our names.
In the breeze, sweet melodies,
Spreading love, igniting flames.

As the sun climbs high and bright,
Hope is woven in the air.
In this moment, pure delight,
Unfettered joy is everywhere.

Dappled Light of Smiles and Serenades

Beneath the trees, the sunlight plays,
Casting shadows in a joyful maze.
Laughter echoes, soft and bright,
A symphony of hearts taking flight.

In gardens where the flowers bloom,
Whispers carried on the breeze's plume.
Every glance a tender song,
In this realm, we all belong.

The dappled light dances around,
As joy and love together are found.
Serenades in the evening air,
Binding hearts with a gentle care.

Moments linger, sweet and pure,
Wrapped in bliss that we endure.
Each smile shared a radiant beam,
In our eyes, the glow of dreams.

So let us bask in this delight,
Underneath the stars so bright.
Together we'll weave our serenades,
In the dappled light, love never fades.

Laughter's Twilight Serenade

As day turns to dusk, the laughter rings,
Carried by breezes on playful wings.
Stars twinkle as the sun dips low,
In twilight's embrace, our spirits grow.

With every chuckle, a spark ignites,
Coloring dreams on soft, velvety nights.
Whispers of joy softly unfold,
In every heartbeat, tales retold.

Under the canopy of evening's blush,
Moments of magic in a gentle hush.
The world slows down, just for a while,
As laughter weaves a heartfelt smile.

Melodies settle in the glowing dark,
A serenade ignited with just a spark.
In this moment, we dance and sway,
Together in twilight, we'll linger and stay.

For in this night, our souls unite,
Guided by laughter, pure and bright.
With each note of joy, we serenade,
The twilight holds our love unafraid.

Rays of Merriment and Dreams

In the morning light, the world awakens,
With rays of joy, the darkness shaken.
Merriment dances in vibrant hues,
A tapestry woven with laughter and views.

Dreams take flight on the wings of dawn,
As we chase visions on shimmering lawns.
Each step we take in radiant cheer,
Filling our hearts, casting out fear.

With smiles that bloom like flowers in spring,
Every moment holds a magical ring.
Together we laugh, create and aspire,
In the warmth of friendship, we never tire.

The sun sets low, painting skies bright,
Guiding our hearts in the fading light.
We gather our dreams in love's embrace,
Celebrating life, in this sacred space.

So let us gather, share our beams,
In rays of merriment, forming our dreams.
For in this glow, we find our way,
Together in joy, come what may.

Reflections of Happiness in Soft Glows

In quiet moments, reflections shine,
Filling our hearts with love divine.
Soft glows linger in the evening air,
A tapestry woven with tender care.

As shadows dance, we share our souls,
In the hush of night, where relaxation rolls.
Each smile mirrors our joyful fate,
In the warmth of friendship, we celebrate.

The stars above ignite the night,
Echoing laughter, pure delight.
In these moments, time stands still,
Every heartbeat, a joyous thrill.

With whispers exchanged, we find our peace,
In gentle glances, our joys increase.
In reflections of happiness, we blend,
Creating a harmony that will never end.

So let us cherish this lovely glow,
In our hearts, let happiness overflow.
For in this calm, our spirits rise,
Reflections of joy beneath the skies.

Curves of Light and Laughter

In the dawn's glow, smiles spread wide,
Where shadows dance, and dreams abide.
Each twinkle tells a joyful song,
Embracing hearts where laughter throngs.

Through whispered winds, we chase the day,
With every step, we find our way.
In every corner, brightness gleams,
Life painted vivid, like our dreams.

Beneath the stars, our secrets blend,
Together, laughter has no end.
As hopes arise with every glance,
We twirl in joy, we take our chance.

With every heartbeat, echoes play,
Life's sweetest notes, we weave and sway.
Curves of light around us bend,
In laughter's arms, we find our friend.

Let shadows fade, let spirits rise,
In this embrace, the world complies.
For in the laughter, light is found,
A harmony that knows no bound.

Season of Happy Laughs

In every corner, joy unfolds,
A season bright with tales retold.
With every giggle, dreams take flight,
Beneath the sun's warm, golden light.

The air is burst with playful cheer,
As friends gather, all hearts near.
With every joke and playful tease,
Laughter flows like a gentle breeze.

Picnics spread on grassy plains,
With bright bouquets and soft refrains.
Each moment cherished, quickly pass,
In the beauty of our happy laughs.

Through playful chimes, the days we share,
In every glance, there's love to spare.
This season warm, as hearts renew,
In the dance of laughter, just we two.

As autumn leaves begin to sway,
We hold these memories, come what may.
A treasure deep of timeless worth,
In this season of laughter and mirth.

Waves of Joyful Embrace

Upon the shoreline, laughter sings,
As waves roll in, their gentle brings.
With every splash, we plunge in deep,
In joyful embrace, our spirits leap.

The sunlight sparkles on the sea,
Where laughter dances, wild and free.
Together we build castles grand,
With hopes and dreams, our hearts expand.

Seagulls call as we run and play,
In this world, trouble fades away.
With every wave that washes ashore,
Joy flows in, bringing us more.

Moments shared like grains of sand,
Scattered wide across the land.
In every hug, in every smile,
We find our bliss, if just for a while.

As twilight falls on the serene bay,
We hold these moments, come what may.
In waves of joy, we find our place,
Wrapped forever in love's embrace.

Portraits of Merriment and Light

In every corner, colors burst,
Creating portraits, a joyful thirst.
Brushes wielded with laughter's thread,
Where memories created, hearts are fed.

With smiles painted in strokes so bold,
Each moment cherished, memories told.
In vibrant hues, the world we see,
A canvas filled with pure glee.

Through the laughter, we find our art,
In friendship's bond, we play our part.
Sketching tales of laughter bright,
Portraits gleaming, pure delight.

As the sun sets, shadows dance,
We capture each other, a playful glance.
In this gallery where love ignites,
We hang our dreams in joyous sights.

In every heartbeat, stories blend,
A tapestry of laughter we send.
These portraits gleam, forever bright,
In the warmth of merriment's light.

Songs of Mirthful Radiance

In fields of gold, the laughter springs,
With every note, the heart takes wing.
The sunbeams dance on gentle streams,
In every mind, a joyful dream.

Sweet melodies weave through the trees,
Whispers carried on the breeze.
A symphony of bright delight,
Chasing shadows from the night.

With every smile, the world glows bright,
Painting colors in soft light.
Songs of mirth that lift the soul,
In harmony, we become whole.

Beneath the sky, our voices blend,
Each sound, a joy that will not end.
Together we laugh, we sing, we play,
In this light, we find our way.

So let us wander, hearts so free,
In the laughter that will always be.
For in the warmth of every cheer,
We'll find our song, forever near.

Threads of Laughter in the Air

A gentle breeze whispers our names,
As laughter twirls in playful games.
Threads of joy weave through the space,
Creating a smile on every face.

In every glance, a spark ignites,
Filling the days with warm delights.
The world around us starts to shine,
In this tapestry, your heart is mine.

Friendly echoes ring through the parks,
As happiness ignites the sparks.
Each giggle flows like rippling streams,
Binding us tight in woven dreams.

Through sunlit paths, we dance and sway,
In the glory of a brightened day.
Laughter lifts us, pure and true,
In every moment shared with you.

So let us gather, hearts laid bare,
Weaving joy in the soft still air.
Threads of laughter will ever stay,
Brightening our joyful play.

Reflections of Timeless Joy

In quiet pools, the laughter gleams,
Echoes of life, like vivid dreams.
Moments captured, forever bright,
Reflections dance in warm sunlight.

From mountain peaks to valleys low,
Our joy flows free, like rivers flow.
In every heartbeat, a story told,
Of timeless laughter, bright and bold.

With friends beside us, hand in hand,
In the beauty of this wondrous land.
We share our secrets, hopes, and fears,
Finding solace in shared cheers.

In every sunrise, a spark of glee,
Painting the sky, setting us free.
Reflections of what brings us joy,
In every girl, in every boy.

So lean into the moments dear,
Hold tight the laughter, keep it near.
For in these echoes, we define,
Reflections bright, forever thine.

Starlit Paths of Playfulness

Beneath the stars, our laughter sings,
Joyful whispers on gentle wings.
Starlit paths invite us to roam,
In the night, we find our home.

With every glance, the magic flows,
Creating wonder as love grows.
In midnight dances, shadows play,
Filling our souls, come what may.

Softly glimmering in the dark,
Each moment shared leaves a mark.
The universe twinkles overhead,
Guiding our dreams where laughter's spread.

Through cosmic fields, we chase the light,
Hand in hand, hearts shining bright.
Playfulness leads our every step,
In this journey, joy is kept.

So let us wander, free and wild,
In the embrace of the cosmic child.
Starlit paths will forever guide,
In laughter's arms, we will abide.

Euphoria's Embrace at Eventide

As daylight fades with gentle grace,
Beneath the sky's warm, glowing face.
The colors blend, a soft delight,
Embracing us into the night.

Joy dances lightly, shadows play,
Whispers of dreams invite us to stay.
In this moment, hearts take flight,
Euphoria glows, a radiant sight.

The world transforms in shades so bright,
As stars awaken, bringing light.
Each breath a gift, each laugh a tune,
We sway beneath the rising moon.

Together, we find our perfect place,
In the soft hush of night's embrace.
With every heartbeat, love ignites,
In euphoria's warmth, our spirits light.

The evening hums a sweet refrain,
A melody that will remain.
As we hold on to this blissful pause,
In gratitude, we count the stars.

Shimmering Laughter Beneath the Moon

Underneath the silver glow,
Laughter dances, soft and slow.
Echoes of joy fill the air,
Bringing warmth beyond compare.

With every giggle, spirits soar,
Hearts are light; they want for more.
The moon above, a watchful friend,
Holds our secrets, hearts to mend.

Stories shared, both old and new,
Woven in dreams that feel so true.
Visions spark with every gleam,
In this night, we dare to dream.

The world retreats as we unite,
Wrapped in laughter, pure delight.
With every glance, a silent tune,
We cherish moments, under moon.

So let the stars guide us, bright,
In the calm embrace of the night.
Together, beneath this celestial dome,
We find a place that feels like home.

Vibrancy in Chimes of Laughter

Laughter rings like bells in spring,
Joyful echoes, hearts take wing.
Each little chuckle, bright and clear,
Bonds us tighter, drawing near.

In vibrant hues, our spirits live,
Sharing warmth that we can give.
With every smile, the world ignites,
A canvas painted with delights.

The air is rich with tales we share,
Moments cherished, love laid bare.
Through timeless paths, our laughter roams,
In friendship's aura, we find homes.

Soft whispers play among the trees,
Carried gently on the breeze.
In this harmony of heart and soul,
Together, we are wonderfully whole.

Embrace the joy, let it be free,
In laughter's chime, we find the key.
For every moment spent in grace,
Is vibrant joy time can't erase.

Glimmers of Joy Beyond the Sunset

As the sun dips low, flames ignite,
Glimmers of joy embrace the night.
In hues of orange, pink, and gold,
A treasure's story begins to unfold.

Each moment shared, a golden thread,
Weaving memories that won't fade.
Underneath the twilight's charm,
We find warmth in each other's arms.

The horizon whispers secrets old,
In shimmering light, our dreams unfold.
With laughter rising, spirits soar,
Beyond the sunset, we crave more.

Stars peek through as shadows fall,
In this quiet, we hear the call.
To cherish life, its wondrous spins,
Where glowing joy eternally begins.

So gather close, and savor now,
In life's embrace, we make a vow.
With glimmers bright beyond the dusk,
We find our strength, in love we trust.

The Dance of Gleeful Spirits

In fields where laughter twirls and spins,
Gleeful spirits sway like winds.
With every turn, the joy they spread,
In a lively dance, where love is bred.

They leap and twirl beneath the sun,
In a symphony that's just begun.
Footfalls soft, like whispers sweet,
They share a rhythm, a heart's heartbeat.

Around the trees, they laugh and sing,
Embracing life, this wondrous spring.
With spirits high and faces bright,
They waltz into the starry night.

Each step a story, a dream anew,
In every glance, a spark of hue.
Their joy, contagious, fills the air,
A dance of souls beyond compare.

Together they dance, forever free,
In the realm of mirth, where hearts agree.
With every spin, they draw us near,
In the dance of spirits, pure and clear.

Illuminated Paths of Silly Dreams

Beneath the glow of a moonlit scheme,
Wander we down the paths of dream.
With laughter bright, we take our flight,
On whimsical trails, painted in light.

Each step a giggle, a joyful sound,
Through enchanted woods, our hearts unbound.
With silly hats and shoes askew,
We leap over shadows, just me and you.

Bubbles of joy float in the air,
As we chase the dreams that dare to share.
Among the stars, our spirits soar,
Illuminated paths, forevermore.

We dance on clouds, we play in streams,
In a world alive with shining beams.
Come join the party, don't be shy,
On these silly paths, let laughter fly.

With every turn, new wonders greet,
The journey's magic, oh, so sweet.
In the heart of night, our dreams ignite,
Illuminated paths, a pure delight.

Twilight's Veil of Joy

As daylight fades, a velvet hush,
Twilight drapes in colors lush.
With gentle hands, it weaves a glow,
A veil of joy, for all to know.

The stars awaken, blink in tune,
While fireflies dance beneath the moon.
In this soft light, we share our dreams,
Wrapped in twilight's tender seams.

The whispers of night, a sweet serenade,
In every shadow, joy will cascade.
Each moment, precious, caught in flight,
Beneath twilight's watchful sight.

With laughter ringing, hearts take flight,
The veil of joy holds us tight.
With every breath, a promise made,
In this twilight, we are unafraid.

So let us savor, this magic hour,
Where dreams are born, and spirits flower.
In twilight's embrace, our souls will sway,
Veils of joy, come what may.

Whirlwinds of Happy Echoes

Around the bend, the echoes play,
A whirlwind dance, come join the fray.
With every laugh, a ripple flows,
In the joy that life bestows.

From hills to valleys, the echoes call,
A symphony of glee that enthralls.
With hearts aglow and spirits bright,
We chase the echoes into the night.

Through meadows wide, hand in hand,
We weave a tapestry, grand and planned.
Each echo a memory, warm and dear,
Whirlwinds of happiness, drawing near.

In the dance of time, we lose our fear,
With every whirl, our hearts draw near.
Where laughter reigns, light shall grow,
In the whirlwind, love will flow.

So let the echoes ring and chime,
In harmony, we share our rhyme.
With every spin, let joy collide,
In whirlwinds of echoes, side by side.

Echoes of Playful Whispers

In the garden, laughter flows,
Softly danced where summer glows.
Tiny feet on dewy grass,
Joyful moments, time does pass.

Whispers low beneath the trees,
Carried gently by the breeze.
Chasing dreams where colors blend,
Echoes play, a sweet pretend.

Fluttering leaves, a playful tune,
Underneath the silver moon.
Secrets shared on slides of gold,
Tales of heart and joy retold.

Giggling children, hearts so free,
Floating high like kites at sea.
In this bliss, we come alive,
In the magic, we all thrive.

As twilight descends, stars appear,
Softly wrapping us in cheer.
In the whispers, dreams take flight,
Echoes dance into the night.

Daughters of Delightful Sunbeams

Radiant rays on fields of gold,
Dance of light, a sight to behold.
Laughter bubbles, spirits rise,
Underneath the vast blue skies.

With flowers woven in their hair,
Girls of sunshine, free as air.
Skipping through the meadow's gleam,
Living life, a vibrant dream.

In every step, the world awakes,
Joyful hearts, the rhythm shakes.
Chasing shadows, secrets share,
In their laughter, love is rare.

A symphony of bright delight,
Guiding stars through endless night.
Daughters of the sun's warm grace,
Shining bright in every place.

Painting skies with hopes anew,
Every wish a vibrant hue.
In their hearts, the future blooms,
Daughters dance through sunlit rooms.

In Celebration of Giggling Hearts

Gather round, the time has come,
To celebrate the joyful hum.
With every giggle, smiles ignite,
Hearts are dancing, pure delight.

In this circle, laughter rings,
Sprinkled joy in simple things.
Bubbles rise and laughter swells,
In each story, magic dwells.

Hopping, skipping, all around,
In this moment, joy is found.
Hearts entwined in playful cheer,
Every giggle holds us near.

As the clouds drift far away,
Sunbeams guide us, light the way.
With each joke, the world feels bright,
In celebration, pure delight.

So raise a glass, let spirits soar,
In giggles shared, we long for more.
Together, our hearts take flight,
In celebration, love ignites.

A Tapestry of Cheerful Shadows

In the evening, shadows play,
Weaving dreams that softly sway.
Colors blend and laughter swirls,
In the night, our joy unfurls.

Moonbeams brush the open glade,
Shimmering hues that light the shade.
Every giggle, every sigh,
Forms a tapestry up high.

Dancing silhouettes of glee,
Whispers shared, wild and free.
In this night, we weave our tales,
Catch the wind, as laughter sails.

Starlit paths beneath our feet,
Every heartbeat, a joyous beat.
With each moment, shadow plays,
In our laughter, love conveys.

As dawn approaches, light will gleam,
In our hearts, a cherished dream.
Together, forever we stand,
A tapestry, hand in hand.

Celestial Humor in the Quiet

Stars chuckle in the dark,
Whispers of night dance mild.
Laughter echoing through space,
A playful cosmos, beguiled.

Moon smiles at the dreaming earth,
Clouds giggle, soft and bright.
Galaxies spin with joy,
In the embrace of the night.

Nebulas weave jokes in color,
Light-years travel with smiles.
Comets crack up as they race,
Winking across many miles.

In silence, the universe jest,
While planets twirl with glee.
A celestial court of humor,
For all, both you and me.

As dawn breaks the quiet spell,
Sunlight tickles the sky,
With every ray, a chuckle,
A cosmic lullaby.

Gleeful Horizons of Heart and Spirit

Sunrise spills joy on the hills,
Colors burst in jubilant cheer.
Winds carry soft laughter's kiss,
Whispers of hope far and near.

Fields stretch in bright green delight,
Each bloom a story to tell.
Hearts dance to the rhythm of life,
In harmony, they swell.

Children's giggles fill the air,
Like bubbles in shimmering light.
Kites soar high, dreams at play,
In the embrace of delight.

Stars dot the twilight canvas,
Filling hearts with gleaming gleam.
Horizons stretch toward the skies,
Where soon all souls can dream.

Evening's warmth wraps the day,
With a promise of peace anew.
In the gleeful heart of the world,
Every spirit finds its view.

A Tapestry of Grins at Dusk

Threads of orange and pink arise,
Weaving bright tales as day fades.
Laughter hangs in the cool air,
As dusk's longing serenades.

Children chase shadows at play,
While crickets begin their song.
Fireflies twinkle in delight,
As night stretches, smooth and long.

Soft whispers blend with the breeze,
In a tapestry spun with joy.
Hope dances on the horizon,
In every girl and boy.

Stars peek through a velvet sky,
Each glowing pinprick a grin.
Night wraps laughter in its arms,
And invites new dreams to begin.

In this quiet hour so sweet,
The world holds its breath in fun.
A tapestry of joy unfolds,
As we wait for the new sun.

Joy's Illumination Beyond Boundaries

Every heart blooms like a flower,
With laughter lighting the way.
Joy spills forth from endless wells,
Chasing the shadows away.

Borders fade with each warm smile,
Cultures meet in radiant grace.
A dance of connections unfolds,
Uniting every embrace.

Through valleys deep and high peaks,
Joy travels, breaking the night.
Embracing all, it knows no walls,
With love as its guiding light.

Even the stillness, it finds a way,
To spark joy in solemn place.
In every silence, a whisper sings,
Hope woven into our space.

Together, we bloom and grow,
In joy's illumination vast.
Beyond boundaries, we gather tight,
Creating bonds that forever last.

Dances of Joyful Radiance

In fields where wildflowers play,
Children dance through golden day.
Laughter echoes in the breeze,
Their hearts entwined with nature's ease.

Underneath a sky so bright,
Joyful spirits take to flight.
Every twirl and spin, a dream,
In this happy, sunny gleam.

Whispers of the daisies sway,
Chasing clouds, they leap and sway.
With each step, their worries fade,
In the warmth of sunlit glade.

Colors splash in vibrant hues,
Joyful moments, nothing to lose.
Every heartbeat sings a song,
In this place where they belong.

As the sun begins to set,
Memories made, they won't forget.
In the twilight's gentle embrace,
Radiant smiles still light their face.

Nimbus of Playful Laughter

A cloud of giggles drifts around,
In every corner, joy is found.
Children playing, spirits high,
As laughter dances in the sky.

Jumping from the grassy hills,
Chasing dreams, the heart fulfills.
Echoes of their joy expand,
Creating magic, hand in hand.

Bubbles float in sunlit air,
Each one holds a whispered care.
In their world, all troubles cease,
Finding joy in every piece.

The breeze carries cheerful sounds,
Laughter woven in the bounds.
Fleeting moments, yet they stay,
In the heart, they softly play.

As day fades to evening's hue,
The laughter sparkles, fresh and new.
In the nimbus of delight,
Their playful spirits take to flight.

Serenities of Blissful Revelry

In twilight's glow, they gather near,
Voices blend, a melody clear.
Together in the soft moonlight,
Hearts entwined, a pure delight.

Tales of joy and dreams unfold,
In the warmth, their hands they hold.
With every word, their spirits rise,
In this moment, joy belies.

The stars above like diamonds shine,
Each twinkling light, a story divine.
Laughter dances in soft chime,
In this revelry of time.

Glimmers of peace in every sigh,
As fireflies twirl in the night sky.
Encircling joy, they find their way,
In blissful revels, they will stay.

With the dawn, they'll rise anew,
Cherishing all that they've been through.
In serenities of the night,
Their souls unite in sheer delight.

Light Beneath the Canvas of Smiles

A palette bright, colors blend,
Underneath the smiles, they send.
With laughter woven through the day,
Each moment sparkles, come what may.

In every giggle, joy resides,
As time flows gently, sweetly glides.
They paint their dreams on fabric wide,
In a tapestry where hearts collide.

Under arches of the sun,
Steps are light, as they all run.
Chasing shadows, bright and free,
In this canvas, joy's decree.

The world may turn, but here they stand,
Joined together, hand in hand.
With laughter echoing each mile,
They find their light beneath the smile.

As twilight dims, their colors blend,
In this joyous world, hearts mend.
Each day a stroke upon the page,
In light beneath, they dance and wage.

The Brightness of Shared Grins

In the garden of laughter, we bloom,
Bright colors dance in every room.
Shared grins light up the dusky sky,
Echoes of joy as moments fly.

With each smile, the shadows fade,
A tapestry of memories made.
Glimmers of hope in every glance,
Our hearts entwined in a joyful dance.

Through trials faced, we stand as one,
Unity shines like the rising sun.
Laughter rings out, pure and true,
In the bright embrace of me and you.

Every chuckle we freely share,
Is a beacon of love, beyond compare.
In the warmth of friendship's glow,
The brightness of shared grins will grow.

So let the world witness our light,
In every day, in every night.
Together we'll cherish this bliss,
Secured forever in every kiss.

Laughter's Gentle Kiss at Dusk

As the sun dips low, the skies ignite,
Laughter whispers softly, a warm delight.
In the twilight's touch, our voices blend,
A gentle reminder that joys transcend.

With every chuckle, darkness retreats,
Life's sweetest moments, where love repeats.
Serenading stars with whispers of cheer,
Laughter's gentle kiss, always near.

With friends beside, the night we embrace,
In this tender moment, find our place.
The horizon glows, a canvas so bright,
Wrapped in laughter, we own the night.

As shadows gather, our spirits soar,
In vibrant echoes, we long for more.
Embracing the dusk, we feel at home,
With laughter's kiss, we'll never roam.

So let us treasure these whispers of grace,
In the twilight's arms, we find our space.
For laughter's gentle kiss is a sweet refrain,
An everlasting melody, never in vain.

Shimmering Waves of Amusement

On the shore where the tide meets the sand,
Shimmering waves bring laughter so grand.
Ripples of joy as they crash and play,
Each splash a song that won't fade away.

Seagulls cry out in a jubilant dance,
Inviting us all to join in the chance.
With each wave that curls, we let out a cheer,
Bubbles of happiness, light as the air.

As the sun dips low, the horizon aglow,
Amusement surrounds us, a radiant show.
In this sea of mirth, we find our delight,
Riding the waves till the fall of night.

With friends by our side, we laugh and we sing,
These shimmering waves forever will bring.
Memories cherished in every embrace,
In the laughter's tide, we find our place.

So let the waves roll, let the joy flow free,
In this world of amusement, you and me.
Together we'll ride every crest, every fall,
In shimmering waves, we will have it all.

Secrets of Joyful Reflections

In the mirror of laughter, we discover light,
Each reflection holds secrets, wondrous and bright.
Moments shared in smiles, stories unfold,
Whispers of joy, as the memories uphold.

In the stillness of evening, with friends gathered near,
We find solace in laughter, dispelling all fear.
Every giggle reveals what our hearts can afford,
Secrets of joy, silently stored.

Through storms of life, we share our fears,
In reflections of laughter, we dry our tears.
The bond of our hearts shines ever so clear,
In the secrets of mirth, we hold each other dear.

So let the echoes of laughter resound,
In joyful reflections, together we're found.
With every shared moment and smile exchanged,
Our secrets of joy will never be estranged.

As the stars appear, our stories align,
In the tapestry woven, your heart next to mine.
Together we'll keep these secrets untold,
In the laughter of life, our joys unfold.

Radiance in Echoes of Joy

In the dawn's first light, we rise,
With laughter woven through the skies,
Each moment bright, pure and clear,
Chasing away the shadows of fear.

Joy springs forth like a gentle stream,
Filling our hearts with a radiant gleam,
In every smile, a story unfolds,
A tapestry of warmth, in hues of gold.

In the fields where wildflowers grow,
With colors that dance, putting on a show,
We gather the echoes of blissful days,
Carving our names in sweet sunlit rays.

From laughter's embrace, we find our way,
Spreading our wings, we learn to play,
The world is alive with each little sound,
In this moment, our joy is unbound.

Beneath the vast skies, we find our place,
In every heart, a warm embrace,
Radiance shines, in each joyful tear,
We share in the echo, drawing near.

Whispers of Glee at Dusk

As the day slips into twilight's embrace,
The whispers of glee fill the space,
Stars begin to twinkle and play,
In the gentle night, worries drift away.

Laughter rings soft like a breeze,
Carrying dreams among the trees,
In the twilight's glow, we come alive,
Finding warmth in each moment we thrive.

With hands held tight, we take a stand,
Lost in the rhythm of a joyous band,
The night unfurls like a velvet sheet,
Celebrating life with every heartbeat.

As shadows stretch and mingle with light,
We dance through the magic of the night,
Each step a whisper, every twirl a song,
In this world of wonder, where we belong.

So here we gather, beneath the stars,
Sharing our secrets, and who we are,
In the quiet dusk, where dreams ignite,
We find our joy, wrapped in the night.

A Symphony of Gleeful Rays

Listen closely to the sun's warm tune,
As it dances high, beneath the moon,
A symphony of joy fills the air,
With every note, banishing care.

Each smile a chord, strummed with delight,
Creating harmony, shining bright,
With laughter cascading like a stream,
In the heart of the night, we chase our dream.

Through fields of laughter, we joyfully roam,
In this symphony, we find our home,
The breezes hum a gentle refrain,
Carrying the echoes of our sweet gain.

We'll sing to the stars with voices pure,
In every whisper, our hearts endure,
As the symphony plays, we sway and spin,
In the melody's warmth, we find within.

So gather around, let the music flow,
In this radiant moment, let your spirit glow,
For in the joy of togetherness, we lay,
A symphony of gleeful rays.

Where Shadows Dance with Delight

In twilight's glow, shadows softly glide,
Whispers of laughter they cannot hide,
As stars awaken, the night takes flight,
Where shadows dance, there's pure delight.

With each flicker, a memory's cast,
In the embrace of night, we hold fast,
The moonlight glimmers, painting our dreams,
In this enchanted realm, nothing is as it seems.

Close your eyes, feel the magic unfold,
In the language of joy, we are bold,
With every heartbeat, a story to share,
In the dance of shadows, we breathe the air.

Together we twirl under starry skies,
In the embrace of night, we rise,
For in the laughter that glimmers bright,
We find our freedom, our shared delight.

So let shadows lead, as we learn to play,
In the moonlit mystery, we'll find our way,
Where joy and shadows gracefully meet,
We'll forever cherish this dance, so sweet.

Echoes from Joy's Lantern

In twilight's glow, laughter spills,
A lantern's flicker, a heart that thrills.
Whispers dance in the warm night air,
Joy's melody sings, free from despair.

Stars auspiciously wink above,
Crafting dreams wrapped in love.
Each moment shared, a radiant thread,
Spinning tales of what lies ahead.

Beneath the glow, we find our way,
The journey brightens with each new day.
Echoes linger, soft and bright,
Guided by joy's gentle light.

Candles flicker, shadows play,
Chasing doubts and fears away.
With every laugh, the spirit lifts,
In joy's embrace, the heart gifts.

As night descends, our spirits soar,
With echoes ringing evermore.
Together we dwell in light's embrace,
Creating memories time can't erase.

Lighthearted Shadows at Dusk

As the sun dips, shadows grow,
In gentle hues, joy starts to flow.
Laughter flutters like a butterfly,
A sweet refrain beneath the sky.

The world wraps in a soft embrace,
A moment held, a sacred space.
Giggles echo in twilight's glow,
Chasing clouds that drift and flow.

Dusk embraces all in sight,
With illusions painted in twilight.
Each smile cast upon the ground,
In vibrant colors, spirits found.

With every step, our shadows blend,
In light's soft touch, our hearts transcend.
Joy dances wildly, free and bright,
Carving memories in the night.

Hand in hand, we stroll with ease,
Finding magic in the evening breeze.
Lighthearted whispers fill the air,
Binding souls with love and care.

Sparks of Uncontainable Delight

In every moment, joy ignites,
With laughter shared, the spirit lights.
Sparks of passion dance and swell,
An uncontainable joy to tell.

Bursting forth like fireworks bright,
Each heartbeat resonating with delight.
Time stands still in this embrace,
A playful smile upon each face.

Chasing dreams like fireflies glow,
Through fields of wonder, we freely flow.
With every cheer, the world expands,
Coloring life with joyful hands.

Moments string like pearls on thread,
Tales of joy and love widespread.
In fleeting glimpses, hearts unite,
In sparks of uncontainable delight.

With laughter's echo through the air,
Life's simple joys beyond compare.
Together, we chase the light anew,
Crafting memories, forever true.

The Canvas of Joyous Echoes

Brushstrokes of laughter fill the air,
On the canvas, joy laid bare.
Every hue tells a story bold,
Whispers of warmth in colors unfold.

The palette shines with vibrant cheer,
A tapestry woven, held so dear.
Images dance like flowers in bloom,
Radiating life, dispelling gloom.

With each stroke, we capture grace,
Painting moments that time can't erase.
Echoes of joy, forever bright,
Illuminate the canvas of life.

Crafting dreams with every blend,
In colors vivid, hearts can mend.
Together we sketch a world anew,
A masterpiece crafted by me and you.

As laughter echoes, shadows fall,
On this canvas, we stand tall.
In joyous strokes, we find our way,
In every heartbeat, love's display.

Luminous Laughter Beneath Starlit Canopies

Underneath the sky's embrace,
Laughter dances with the stars,
Whispers of joy find their place,
Painting dreams in evening hours.

Secrets shared in gentle light,
Nature listens to our bliss,
Night unfolds its soft delight,
In the dark, we find our kiss.

Fireflies twinkle, hearts align,
Echoes brush the moonlit ground,
Every giggle feels divine,
In this space, love's warmth is found.

Beneath the canopy we stay,
Wrapped in laughter's sweet embrace,
As the stars begin to play,
In this moment, time slows pace.

With every chuckle, spirits soar,
In the night, we feel alive,
Luminous laughter evermore,
Together here, we'll always thrive.

Echoes of Elation in Twilight

The sun dips low, the sky aglow,
Colors bleed into the night,
Echoes of laughter softly flow,
Stirring hearts with pure delight.

In twilight's arms, we gather near,
Sharing dreams and hopes anew,
Elated voices, bright and clear,
Sing of skies in vibrant hue.

The whispers of the evening breeze,
Mingle with our joyous song,
Every moment, it's a tease,
In this place, we all belong.

As shadows stretch and stars appear,
We hold each other ever tight,
With laughter, we will conquer fear,
Painting twilight with our light.

In these echoes, joy will bloom,
A symphony of hearts in tune,
Filling space, dispelling gloom,
As we dance beneath the moon.

The Dawn of Joyful Whispers

As dawn unfurls her golden wings,
Soft whispers drift upon the air,
The world awakens, nature sings,
In the light, we begin to share.

With every ray, joy starts to grow,
Filling hearts with warmth and cheer,
The gentle breeze begins to blow,
Calling us to gather near.

Hand in hand, we greet the day,
With laughter echoing through the trees,
In this moment, worries fray,
As we savor, minds at ease.

Every smile a precious spark,
Lighting up the morning bright,
Through shadows, we'll leave our mark,
In the glow of morning light.

Together here, we will create,
Joyful whispers, tales to weave,
In the dawn, we celebrate,
A world where love will never leave.

Celestial Chuckles on the Breeze

Under skies where stardust swirls,
Echoes of laughter softly rise,
Celestial chuckles interlace,
With the whispers of the skies.

As we wander through the night,
Glimmers of joy twinkle bright,
In this space, our spirits take flight,
Floating on stars, pure delight.

The winds carry our glee afar,
Beneath a canopy of dreams,
Each chuckle shines like a star,
In the dark, hope brightly beams.

With every breeze, new tales unfold,
Tales of love, cherished and true,
In every giggle, warmth we hold,
Finding magic in the blue.

Underneath the vast expanse,
Together we shall always stay,
In the night, we share our dance,
Celestial chuckles lead the way.

Luminous Jests Beneath the Stars

Beneath the vast and twinkling night,
Laughter dances, pure delight.
Whispers softly on the breeze,
Joyful hearts afloat with ease.

Stars above like winking eyes,
Glimmering with playful sighs.
Every chuckle a bright spark,
Lighting up the endless dark.

In the silence, giggles swell,
Stories woven, all is well.
Underneath this cosmic dome,
Finding warmth, we feel at home.

Echoes of mirth play around,
In this space, our dreams are found.
A tapestry of laughter spun,
Unity with each setting sun.

So let the night be filled with fun,
As we dance till day is done.
In the glow of silver beams,
We nurture all our hopeful dreams.

When Laughter Paints the Sky

When laughter spills like gentle rain,
Colors burst through joy and pain.
Sunset hues in vibrant sway,
Moments of mirth, they brightly play.

Clouds like canvases up high,
Brushstrokes mixed as we comply.
Every giggle, every grin,
Crafting stories from within.

With every joke, the world awakes,
In our hearts, a spark it makes.
Painting skies with hues of gold,
A symphony of joy unfolds.

Together, we create this art,
A masterpiece from every heart.
When laughter paints the sky above,
We write our tale of hope and love.

So share your smiles, let them shine,
Like twinkling stars they intertwine.
Each ray of bliss, a treasured sigh,
When laughter breathes, we learn to fly.

Everlasting Rays of Cheer

In a world of fleeting glances,
Everlasting joy advances.
Sunlight streaming through the trees,
Sparking laughter on the breeze.

Moments linger, bright and bold,
Stories shared and hearts unfold.
Radiant smiles on every face,
Finding warmth in every place.

Together we lift spirits high,
Underneath the endless sky.
Each ray a whisper, soft and clear,
We bask in the warmth of cheer.

Boundless joy, like waves, we ride,
In this ocean, side by side.
Hand in hand, we chase the light,
An embrace of pure delight.

Everlasting moments we'll hold dear,
Written with laughter, free from fear.
In every heart, a spark will stay,
Illuminating every day.

Melodies of Mirth and Light

With every note, our spirits soar,
Melodies of joy we explore.
In harmony, we find our place,
Laughter brightens every space.

The rhythm of the night unfolds,
Tales of happiness retold.
Voices rise, like birds in flight,
Singing songs of sheer delight.

A dance of dreams beneath the moon,
Every smile a sweet commune.
In this concert of our souls,
We discover how love unfolds.

As symphonies entwine and play,
Moments cherished, come what may.
The world aglow with every tune,
Together, we rise, a joyous moon.

In laughter's embrace, we unite,
Melodies of mirth ignite.
Let's weave a tapestry so bright,
With love and light, we take flight.

Horizon of Laughter's Embrace

At dawn we dance on golden shores,
With laughter echoing evermore.
The waves bring joy, a rhythmic beat,
In friendship's arms, our hearts are sweet.

Beneath the sky, we chase the sun,
Every smile shared, a thread we've spun.
With every joke, the shadows fade,
In this embrace, our fears betrayed.

The horizon beams, a canvas bright,
Where echoes of giggles cut the night.
Each moment cherished, held up high,
A truly shared laugh never dies.

In whispered tales of days gone by,
We weave a tapestry, you and I.
Together we find the light we seek,
In laughter's hold, we're never meek.

With every heartbeat, joy unconfined,
In laughter's embrace, peace we find.
Forward we march, hand in hand,
On this horizon, forever we stand.

Twilight's Heartfelt Laughter

The sun dips low, a golden hue,
In twilight's glow, our laughter grew.
Stories shared under starlit skies,
With every giggle, the world complies.

Fireflies dance, a whimsical crew,
In the breeze, our spirits flew.
The night wraps us in gentle glee,
Where laughter flows, and hearts are free.

Whispers soft, like dreams that glide,
In this moment, we'll never hide.
Each chuckle brightens the dusky air,
A heartfelt bond beyond compare.

We twirl and spin, shadows in play,
In laughter's embrace, we find our way.
The night unfolds, a tapestry fine,
With every grin, our souls align.

In twilight's heart, we find our place,
An endless realm of warm embrace.
With every laugh, we weave a song,
In this dance of joy, we belong.

Gleaming Moments of Merriment

In quiet corners, laughter glows,
A spark ignites where friendship flows.
Each giggle a gem, precious and rare,
In fleeting moments, we lay our care.

The sun peeks through, a golden gleam,
In shared laughter, we chase the dream.
With every jest, our spirits lift,
These gleaming moments are the gift.

Around the table, stories entwine,
With hearty laughter, hearts combine.
Each memory crafted, each tale adored,
In these moments, worries ignored.

We chase the dusk, the joy we find,
In every smile, our hearts aligned.
Gleaming moments light the way,
In laughter's warmth, we choose to stay.

The world may spin, yet here we keep,
These moments of mirth, forever steep.
In bonds of laughter, we rejoice,
In every chuckle, we find our voice.

A Symphony of Radiant Giggles

In the garden of joy, laughter sings,
A symphony bright, on playful wings.
With each radiant giggle, the world awakes,
A dance of delight, as starlight shakes.

Notes of joy in the morning air,
In every corner, laughter's fair.
The melody weaves through trees so tall,
A harmony sweet, a clarion call.

As the sun dips low, hues intertwine,
We join the chorus, spirits shine.
Every chuckle an echo, a vibrant spark,
In this symphony, we leave our mark.

Together we rise, on laughter's breeze,
Each radiant giggle, a moment to seize.
With joy as our guide, and hearts aligned,
In this playful song, true love we find.

As nighttime falls, the stars will play,
A symphony of giggles leads the way.
In the warmth of friendship, forever we stay,
In this radiant music, we dance and sway.

A Journey to the Island of Laughs

On the waves of joy we sail,
With laughter in our hearts so pale.
Jokes and smiles the winds do blow,
To the island where the giggles grow.

Seas of chuckles, shores of cheer,
In this haven, we have no fear.
Under palm trees, laughter rings,
As the sun shines bright on playful things.

Every wave a joke to share,
Every breeze, a moment rare.
Skimming stones that waltz and play,
On this island, we find our way.

With every step upon the sand,
Laughter echoes, perfectly planned.
Dancing shadows, free and light,
As the day turns into night.

So let our journey never end,
To the island where we blend.
With joy, our compass, pure and true,
A journey shared by me and you.

Bright Horizons of Friendly Glee

In the morning light we rise,
With joyful hearts and shining skies.
Waves of laughter greet the dawn,
In this land where worries yawn.

Each corner holds a friendly face,
With hugs and smiles, we find our place.
Bright horizons call to me,
Come join the dance, wild and free.

Laughter bubbles like a stream,
In every moment, we find a dream.
Together we can paint the day,
With colors bright in every way.

Underneath the sun's warm glow,
In circles of friends, love will flow.
With every giggle, every cheer,
We build a world that draws us near.

So step into this joyful scene,
Where every heart knows what we mean.
In blessings rich, our spirits leap,
In friendly glee, our souls we keep.

Twilight Whispers of Happiness

As the sun dips low with grace,
Twilight whispers, a soft embrace.
Stars begin to twinkle bright,
Guiding us through the velvet night.

In the hush, our laughter glows,
In every shadow, fondness grows.
Stories shared beneath the sky,
In this moment, we learn to fly.

Moonlit pathways, soft and clear,
Every heartbeat draws us near.
With whispers of joy, we stroll,
In twilight's arms, we feel whole.

The world fades softly, dimmed by stars,
In this twilight, we forget scars.
With gentle laughter in the air,
We weave our dreams without a care.

So let the night unfold its charms,
In each embrace, with open arms.
Together we'll dance through the haze,
In twilight whispers, endless praise.

Light That Twinkles With Laughter

In the evening, laughter glows,
Like twinkling stars, the joy bestows.
Moments spark like fireflies,
In the dark, our spirit flies.

Every giggle casts a beam,
Creating memories that gleam.
As the night plays its sweet song,
We find where our hearts belong.

Dancing shadows, soft and spry,
In the glow, we learn to fly.
With every chuckle, every cheer,
Laughter's light draws us near.

Here, the world feels warm and bright,
In the embrace of soft moonlight.
With friends beside and joy all around,
In every heartbeat, laughter's found.

So let us cherish every laugh,
In this glow, we find the path.
With twinkling light upon our way,
We celebrate life, come what may.

Radiance of Shared Happiness

In the glow of morning light,
Friends gather, hearts so bright.
Laughter dances in the air,
Moments cherished, beyond compare.

Fields of joy, where dreams collide,
United spirits, side by side.
Echoes of bliss, soft and true,
Radiant smiles, our bond anew.

In shared stories, we find peace,
A tapestry of love that won't cease.
Each word a stitch, each laugh a thread,
Woven together, as joy is spread.

Through trials faced, we stand as one,
Together shining, like the sun.
Hope ignites in every glance,
In this sweet, eternal dance.

So let us bask in this embrace,
The warmth of friends, a sacred place.
With radiant hearts, our spirits rise,
In shared happiness, our true prize.

Flickers of Joy in the Breeze

As daylight breaks, the world awakes,
Joy flutters soft, like waves in lakes.
Whispers of laughter through the trees,
   Carried gently by playful breeze.

Children's giggles, an echoing sound,
In gardens where magic knows no bound.
With every flutter, hopes take flight,
   Flickers of joy, bold and bright.

In warm sunlight, friendships bloom,
   Sprinkling love, dispelling gloom.
Hands held tight, we chase the day,
   And let our spirits freely play.

Moments captured, like fireflies' glow,
In the twilight, our hearts do flow.
Together we dance, under the sky,
   Flickers of joy, as if to fly.

So chase the breezes, wild and free,
Life's simple treasures, for you and me.
Let joy's embrace forever please,
   In the flickers, find our ease.

Laughter's Serenade Beneath the Moon

Beneath the pale and silvery light,
We gather close, hearts feeling bright.
Laughter's echoes, a soothing song,
In the night, where we belong.

With every chuckle, the stars align,
Moments shared, pure and divine.
In whispers soft, our secrets flow,
Brighter than constellations' glow.

Moonlit paths where dreams are cast,
United in joy, we hold steadfast.
With every grin, our spirits soar,
Laughter's serenade, we crave for more.

As shadows dance and time stands still,
In warmth of friendship, hearts do fill.
Together we weave our tales in song,
In the moonlight, where we belong.

So let us linger in this delight,
With laughter's serenade, through the night.
Hand in hand, let worries cease,
In the magic, find our peace.

Glistening Trails of Kindred Spirits

On trails where friendships intertwine,
Glistening paths, a journey so fine.
Each step we take, side by side,
In kindred spirits, our hearts abide.

Through valleys deep and mountains high,
Laughter reflects in the open sky.
Memories echo, sweet and clear,
Guiding us forward, year after year.

In each heartbeat, a tale unfolds,
Of shared adventures, brave and bold.
Together we wander, hand in hand,
Creating magic in this land.

Every sunset paints our dreams,
While glistening stars weave silver beams.
Kindred spirits, forever true,
In trails of light, we see the new.

So let us cherish this wondrous quest,
With open hearts, we are truly blessed.
In glistening trails, we find our fate,
Where love and laughter celebrate.

Burst of Joyful Whispers

Whispers flutter in the air,
Carried on the morning breeze,
Soft laughter everywhere,
Dancing among the leafy trees.

Colors burst from dawn's light,
Painting dreams on waking eyes,
Every moment, pure delight,
Underneath the brightening skies.

Clouds drift softly like a sigh,
Day unfolds, a joyful tale,
Echoes of a sweet goodbye,
In the wind, the hopes set sail.

Hearts unite in radiant cheer,
Hand in hand, they sway and spin,
Each note ringing loud and clear,
Crisp and fresh like spring's begin.

In this world of shining grace,
We weave memories, bright and bold,
Joyful whispers find their place,
A tapestry of stories told.

Silhouettes of Gleeful Spirits

Silhouettes dance in twilight's glow,
Fleeting forms that laugh and play,
With each step, the shadows flow,
Magic lingers as they sway.

Chasing dreams on silver beams,
Underneath the starry night,
Launching hopes like whispered themes,
As the moon ignites their flight.

Every heart a vibrant beat,
Together in the lively chase,
With every rhythm, joy's complete,
Life's a lovely, fast embrace.

Framing moments rich and warm,
In the dance, we find our role,
Gleeful spirits take the form,
Filling up the serenade of soul.

Echoes linger, soft and clear,
As night fades into day's hue,
Gleeful spirits, ever near,
Whispering the magic true.

Rainbows of Happy Thoughts

After rain, the colors bloom,
Bright and bold, a vivid sweep,
Painting skies and chasing gloom,
Where the heart takes joyful leaps.

Thoughts like rainbows arching high,
Curving smiles from side to side,
In our minds, they float and fly,
Where happiness cannot hide.

Threads of laughter in the air,
Woven between the clouds divine,
Joyful moments, light as air,
In our hearts, a spark will shine.

Gathering like drops of dew,
Every thought begins to blend,
Colors burst, a vibrant hue,
In the joy that never ends.

Sunrise brings the brightest song,
Wraps the world in hues so bright,
With each note, we all belong,
In a dance that feels so right.

Brilliance Wrapped in Joy

Twilight wraps the day in gold,
As stars peek from a velvet cloak,
Laughter spills, a tale retold,
In every word, the heart awoke.

Moments spark like fireflies' glow,
Filling nights with gleeful light,
Each memory begins to flow,
Guiding souls through endless flight.

Brilliance shines in every glance,
Tie the threads of dreams we weave,
Wrapped in warmth, we take a chance,
In the joy, we believe.

As the sun dips below the line,
Colors fade yet stay alive,
In our hearts, a sparkle shines,
For in joy, we thrive and strive.

Today's whispers carry on,
Echoes of a life well-played,
In brilliance, dusk turns to dawn,
Wrapped in joy, we're not afraid.